Mary Jones, Diane Fellowes-Freeman and Michael Smyth

Cambridge Checkpoint
Science

Challenge Workbook

9

CAMBRIDGE
UNIVERSITY PRESS

Introduction

Welcome to the Cambridge Checkpoint Science Challenge Workbook 9

The Cambridge Checkpoint Science course covers the Cambridge Secondary 1 Science curriculum framework. The course is divided into three stages: 7, 8 and 9.

You should use this Challenge Workbook with Coursebook 9 and Workbook 9. The tasks in this Challenge Workbook will help you to develop and extend your skills and understanding in science. This workbook is offered as extension to the main curriculum and therefore it does not cover all the curriculum framework content for this stage.

The tasks will challenge you with scientific enquiry skills, such as planning investigations, interpreting and analysing results, forming conclusions and discussing them.

They will also challenge you to **apply** your knowledge to answer questions that you have not seen before, rather than just recall that knowledge.

If you get stuck with a task:

Read the question again and look carefully at any diagrams, to find any clues.

Think carefully about what you already know **and** how you can use it in the answer.

Look up any words you do not understand in the glossary at the back of the Checkpoint Science Coursebook, or in your dictionary.

Read through the matching section in the Coursebook. Look carefully at the diagrams there too.

Check the reference section at the back of the Coursebook. There is a lot of useful information there.

Introducing the learners

Nor   Amal   Sam

Anna   Elsa   Jon

Unit 1 Plants

1.1 Floating discs experiment

This challenge task relates to **1.1 Photosynthesis** from the Coursebook.

> In this challenge task, you will interpret the results of an experiment. You will think about variables, write a conclusion and use your scientific knowledge to explain a set of results.

Elsa and Nor do an experiment to investigate photosynthesis.

They cut ten little discs out of a leaf, using a hole punch. Each disc is exactly the same size and is cut from the same leaf.

They put one disc into water in a small beaker and shine light onto it.

Little bubbles appear on the underside of the leaf disc.

After a while, the bubbles of gas make the leaf disc float to the surface of the water.

Elsa and Nor record the time taken for the leaf disc to float to the surface, then repeat their experiment with four more leaf discs.

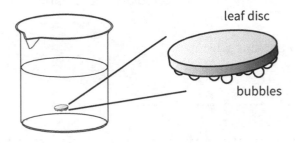

leaf disc

bubbles

1 Name the gas that the leaf disc produced when it photosynthesised.

....

2 Explain why the bubbles of gas formed on the underside of the leaf, not on the top.

....

....

3 In what way does the time taken for the leaf disc to rise depend on the bubbles of gas? Explain your answer.

....

....

....

Elsa and Nor do the investigation again, but this time they put the beaker and the leaf discs in a room with all the lights turned off.

Here are the girls' results.

Conditions	Time taken for leaf disc to rise to the surface / s					
	Try 1	Try 2	Try 3	Try 4	Try 5	Mean
bright light	14	3	12	14	11	
dim light	44	66	69	77	71	

4 Suggest the question that the girls were testing.

....

....

5 What was the **independent variable** in the girls' experiment?

....

6 Elsa thought that there was one **anomalous** result in each row of their results table.

Draw circles around the **two** anomalous results in the table.

> Remember not to include the anomalous results when you calculate the mean.

7 Calculate the **mean** times taken for each row in the results table, and write them in the last column.

8 Suggest why the times taken for the five leaf discs to rise in each of the lighting conditions were not all the same.

....

....

....

....

9 Write a **conclusion** for the girls' experiment.

....

....

10 Suggest an **explanation** for the difference between the mean times for the leaf discs to rise in bright light and in dim light.

....

....

....

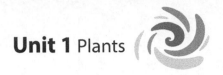

1.2 Van Helmont's experiment

This challenge task relates to **1.3 Plants and water** from the Coursebook.

> In this challenge task, you will look at the work of one of the first people to do scientific experiments, about 350 years ago. Then you will imagine you are this person and think about how to test your ideas.

Johannes Baptista van Helmont was born in Belgium in 1580. In 1648, he set up an experiment to try to find out what a willow plant uses to help it to grow.

> A pound is an old unit of measuring mass. One pound is just under half a kilogram.

Van Helmont cut a shoot from a willow tree and weighed it. He found that it weighed 5 pounds.

He dried some soil, weighed out 200 pounds of it, and put it into a very big pot. He sank the pot into the ground, and then planted the willow shoot in the soil. He covered the soil in the pot with a metal cover, with small holes to let water in.

Over the next five years, van Helmont watered the willow plant whenever the soil got dry. Each autumn, the leaves fell off the plant, and new ones grew in the spring.

After five years, he dug up the tree and weighed it again. He found that it weighed more than 169 pounds. He collected all of the soil in the pot, dried it, and weighed it. Its mass was just under 200 pounds.

He did not weigh the leaves that fell off the plant each autumn.

1 Describe what van Helmont did well in his experiment.

....

....

....

....

....

2 Describe how van Helmont could have improved his experiment.

....

....

....

....

....

> Do not suggest other experiments he could have done; just suggest how he could have made **this** experiment better.

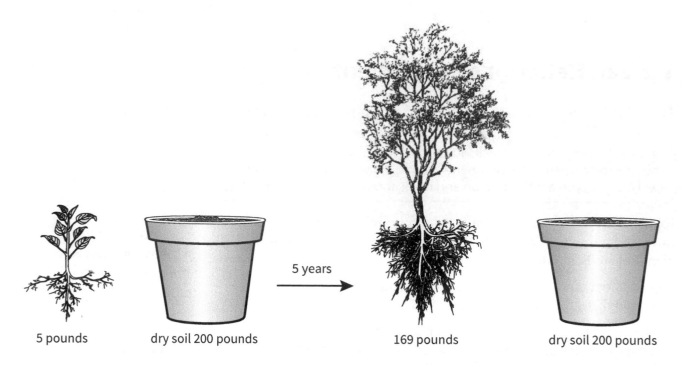

5 pounds   dry soil 200 pounds   5 years   169 pounds   dry soil 200 pounds

In 1648, no one knew anything about photosynthesis. Also, it was very rare for people to do scientific experiments to try to find answers to questions. No one had really worked out how to plan good experiments.

Van Helmont's conclusion was that 164 pounds of wood, bark and roots were produced from water alone.

3 Suggest how van Helmont's reasoning led to this conclusion.

....

....

....

....

....

4 Use your knowledge about photosynthesis to explain why van Helmont's conclusion was wrong.

....

....

....

....

....

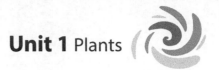

Van Helmont did know that there were gases in the air. In other experiments, he discovered carbon dioxide, which he called 'sylvestre'. He knew that 'sylvestre' was present in the gases produced when yeast ferments, and when charcoal was burnt. (Charcoal is made from wood.) However, it seems he did not link this knowledge to his willow tree experiment.

5 Imagine you are van Helmont. You have suddenly realised that the reason charcoal gives off 'sylvestre' when it is burnt might be because the tree took in 'sylvestre' as it grew. You have an idea that perhaps some of the increase in mass of the willow shoot was because it took in 'sylvestre' as it grew.

This is a difficult challenge. Discuss your ideas with others before you plan what to write.

Describe an experiment that you could do, as van Helmont and in the time that he lived, to see if your idea is correct.

....

....

....

....

....

....

....

....

....

....

....

....

....

....

....

....

1.3 The life cycle of a flowering plant

This challenge task relates to **1.4 Flowers, 1.5 Pollination** and **1.6 Fertilisation** from the Coursebook.

> In this challenge task, you will bring together what you have learnt about the parts, the life and the reproduction of a flowering plant.

The first diagram shows the life cycle of a flowering plant. The lower diagrams show three of the stages in this life cycle.

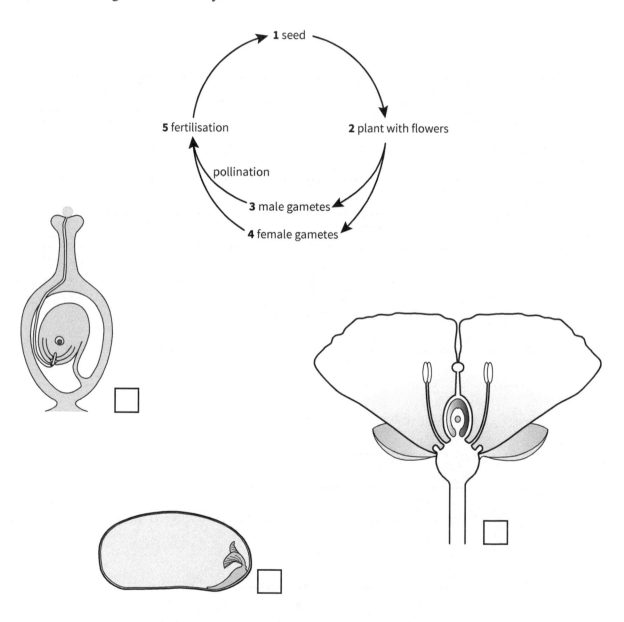

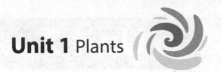

1 Look at the life cycle diagram on the previous page.

   Decide which numbered stage of the life cycle is shown in the other diagrams.
   Write the number from the life cycle diagram in the box next to the diagram that
   illustrates that stage.

2 Here are some descriptions of plant parts.

   For each one, write the name of the part that is being described.

   A Male gametes are made here. ....

   B Female gametes are made here. ....

   C This protects the seed while it is waiting to germinate. ....

   D These parts attract insects to the flower. ....

   E This will grow into a new plant when the seed germinates. ....

   F This will develop into a seed after fertilisation is completed. ....

   G This receives pollen grains, which may have been brought by a bee. ....

   H This is where pollen grains are made. ....

   I This fuses with a female gamete to produce a zygote. ....

   J This will develop into a fruit as the seeds form inside it. ....

3 Now use the letters above to label the diagrams opposite.

   > You may want to use more than one letter for some
   > parts of the diagrams.
   >
   > You may want to use each letter more than once.
   >
   > Use label lines for your labels. Do not write on top
   > of the diagrams.

2.1 Investigating algae on a tree trunk

This challenge task relates to **2.3 Ecology** from the Coursebook.

> In this challenge task, you will think about the design of an ecology experiment, and how to display and interpret the results.

Amal and Jon noticed that the trunks of the trees growing outside their school had green organisms growing on them.

Their teacher told them these were algae, which are very small plant-like organisms.

I think there are more algae on the shady, north-facing sides of the tree trunks than on the sunniest sides.

Where Amal and Jon live (in the northern hemisphere), north-facing surfaces receive the least sunlight and south-facing surfaces receive the most.

The boys decided to collect data to decide whether Amal's idea was correct. This is what they did:

- They chose five trees growing in the same area.
- They cut out a square piece of transparent plastic with sides of 10 cm.
- They very carefully drew a 1 cm grid on the plastic.
- They tied a string horizontally around the first tree trunk, exactly 1.5 m up from the ground.
- They attached the grid to the string, on the north-facing side of the tree trunk.
- They counted how many squares had algae in them.
- Then they moved the grid along the string to the east-facing side, and counted again.
- They repeated this on the south-facing and west-facing sides.
- They did this for each of the five trees.

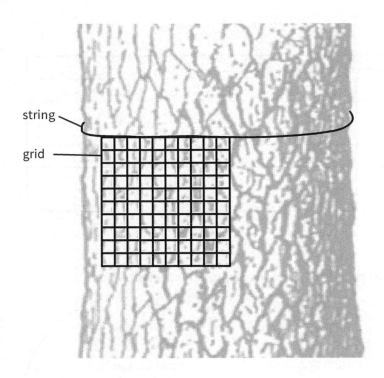

string

grid

1 Describe how the boys could check which is the north-facing side of the tree.

....

....

2 Explain why it was a good idea to tie a string around each tree at 1.5 m above
the ground.

....

....

....

....

3 Explain why it was a good idea to use a grid that was 10 cm × 10 cm, rather than
a larger one or a smaller one.

....

....

....

....

Here are the boys' results.

Tree	Number of squares containing algae			
	Facing north	Facing east	Facing south	Facing west
1	89	39	17	54
2	75	43	29	51
3	96	36	46	60
4	33	12	2	15
5	72	38	12	48

The boys discussed what to plot on a graph to display their results.

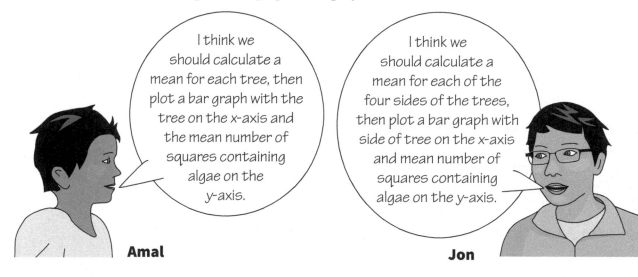

I think we should calculate a mean for each tree, then plot a bar graph with the tree on the x-axis and the mean number of squares containing algae on the y-axis.

Amal

I think we should calculate a mean for each of the four sides of the trees, then plot a bar graph with side of tree on the x-axis and mean number of squares containing algae on the y-axis.

Jon

4 Who was right? Explain your answer.

....

....

....

5 Complete the results chart above in the way that you have decided is best.

6 Use your results to draw a bar chart on the grid.

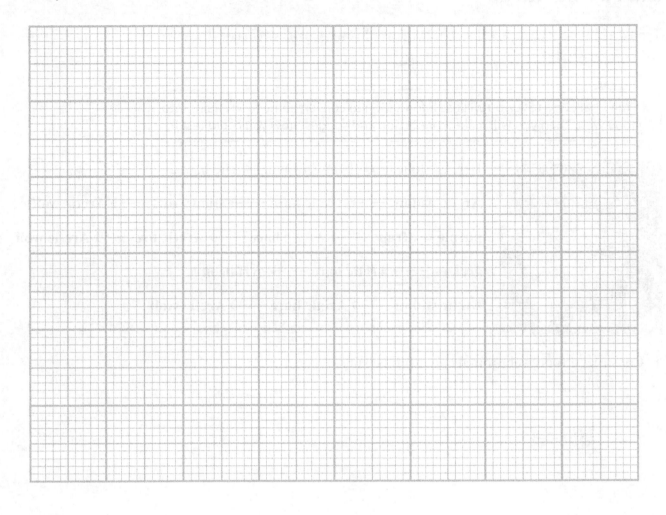

7 Write a conclusion for the boys' experiment.

....

....

....

8 Suggest an explanation for the pattern shown in the results.

....

....

....

2.2 Arctic hares

This challenge task relates to **2.4 Food webs and energy flow** from the Coursebook.

> In this challenge task, you will use information to convert some food chains into a food web. Then you will make a prediction and suggest how you could test it.

An Arctic hare

Here are four food chains involving Arctic hares.

Arctic willow ⟶ Arctic hare ⟶ snowy owl ⟶ Arctic wolf

purple saxifrage ⟶ Arctic hare ⟶ Arctic fox ⟶ Arctic wolf

grasses ⟶ Arctic hare ⟶ gyrfalcon

Arctic willow ⟶ Arctic hare ⟶ Arctic wolf

1 Construct a food web from the four food chains.

2 Some places in the Arctic have fewer willows, purple saxifrage and grasses than other areas.

Predict how the numbers of these plants would affect the number of Arctic hares.

....

....

Explain your prediction.

....

....

....

....

3 Suggest how you could use **sampling techniques** to test your prediction.

Below and on the next page, describe:

• the data you would collect

• how you would collect your data

• how you would record and display your data.

> You could estimate the number of Arctic hares living in an area by counting the number of piles of faeces (droppings).

....

....

....

....

....

....

....

....

....

....

....

2 Living things in their environment

2.3 Predator and prey populations

This challenge task relates to **2.6 Populations** from the Coursebook.

> In this challenge task, you will interpret a complex graph. You will use evidence from the graph to evaluate a suggestion, and then make more suggestions yourself.

Wolves are predators. In some parts of North America, one of their main prey is young moose.

A young moose

The graph shows the numbers of wolves and moose in one region, between 1959 and 2011.

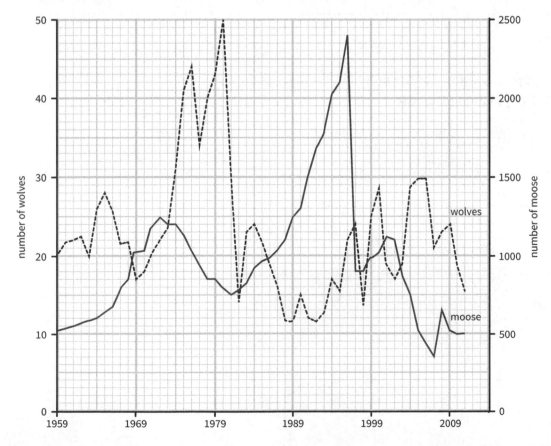

1 What was the highest number of wolves during this period, and in what year did this occur?

....

2 What was the highest number of moose during this period, and in what year did this occur?

....

3 A scientist suggested that the number of wolves affects the number of moose.

Explain how the graph on the previous page provides evidence that supports this suggestion.

....

....

....

....

....

....

....

4 Explain how the graph indicates that the number of wolves is not the only factor affecting the population of moose.

....

....

....

....

....

5 Suggest **two** factors, other than the size of the moose population, that might affect the number of wolves.

....

....

6 Suggest **two** factors, other than the size of the wolf population, that might affect the number of moose.

....

....

Unit 3 Variation and inheritance

3.1 Constructing a key

This challenge task relates to **3.1 Keys** from the Coursebook.

> In this challenge task, you will construct a key to help someone to identify a leaf.

The pictures show leaves from five different plants.

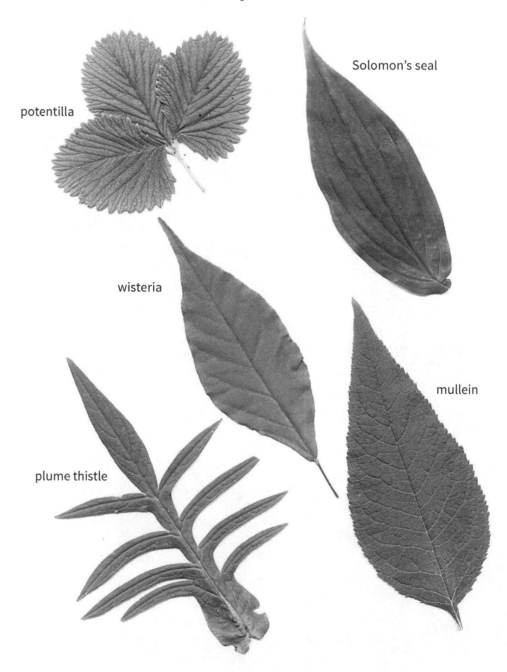

potentilla

Solomon's seal

wisteria

plume thistle

mullein

1 Make a list of **six** ways in which the leaves differ from each other.

....

....

....

2 Write a **key** to help someone to identify these leaves.

The key needs to work when the person has only one leaf, with no others to compare it with.

3.2 The world's most famous sheep

This challenge task relates to **3.3 Inheritance** and **3.4 More about inheritance** from the Coursebook.

> In this challenge task, you will use some new scientific information, presented as a series of bullet points, to construct a flow chart. You do not need to remember this information – the purpose of the task is to change information presented in words into a flow chart.

On 5 July 1996, scientists were very excited when a lamb was born. She was named Dolly. She was special because she was the first mammal to be born as a result of a new technique, called nuclear transfer.

This is how Dolly came into the world:

- Scientists took a cell from the body of a female sheep with a white face. They removed the nucleus from the cell.
- Then they took an egg cell from a female sheep with a black face. They removed the nucleus from this egg cell, and replaced it with the nucleus from the sheep with a white face.
- They put the egg cell into a Petri dish and gave it a small electric shock to make it start dividing.
- When the egg cell had produced a little ball of several cells – an embryo – they put it into the uterus of the sheep with a black face.
- The pregnant sheep gave birth to Dolly.

1 Construct a **flow chart** on the next page to explain clearly how Dolly was produced. You could include some drawings.

If you like, you could find more information about Dolly on the internet and add some of this to your flow chart, but make sure it is all easy for someone to understand.

> A flow chart has simple statements, linked by arrows, to show a sequence of events or processes. It can include illustrations.

Draw your flow chart here.

Dolly

2 Think about how features are passed on from parents to offspring. Explain why Dolly had a white face, and not a black face.

Look in your Coursebook if you need some reminders.

....

....

....

....

3 Usually, a young animal inherits a mixture of features from its mother and its father. Do you think Dolly inherited a mixture of features? Explain your answer.

....

....

....

....

3.3 Breeding goats in Ethiopia

This challenge task relates to **3.5 Selective breeding** from the Coursebook.

> In this challenge task, you will use your understanding of selective breeding to advise Ethiopian farmers how they can improve their herds of goats.

Many farmers in Ethiopia keep goats to provide their families with milk and meat.

A study was carried out to investigate how farmers choose which goats to breed from. Scientists gave questionnaires to 306 households in one part of Ethiopia.

They found that 72% of the farmers simply allowed any of the goats in the herd to breed together.

The other 28% of farmers chose female and male goats with certain characteristics for breeding. The tables below show the five characteristics that these farmers considered most important when choosing which goats they allowed to breed.

Feature of female goats	Importance (1 = high, 5 = low)
number of offspring produced in one year	1
growth rate	2
age when first became able to get pregnant	3
appearance (other than colour)	4
disease resistance	5

Feature of male goats	Importance (1 = high, 5 = low)
growth rate	1
appearance (other than colour)	2
colour	3
disease resistance	4
family history of the goat	5

1 Which characteristics did the farmers look for in **both** female and male goats, when choosing which ones to breed together?

....

....

....

2 Suggest why the most important five features listed are not all the same for female and male goats.

....

....

....

....

3 Think about how farmers in Ethiopia could improve their herds of goats by selective breeding.

Use the information on the previous page to remind yourself what the farmers are doing now and why they keep goats.

Then, below and on the next page, construct a message to the farmers to help them to improve their herds.

Your message could be in words, or in drawings, or a mix of both.

....
....
....
....
....
....
....
....
....
....
....
....
....
....
....
....
....
....
....
....
....
....
....

3.4 Bringing Darwin up to date

This challenge task relates to **3.8 Charles Darwin** from the Coursebook.

> In this challenge task, you will first summarise Darwin's theory of natural selection in your own words, and then explain how our knowledge of chromosomes and genes supports this theory.

1 Write a series of short sentences to **summarise** Darwin's theory of natural selection.

Include these words in your summary:

adapted   **inherit**   **survive**   **reproduce**   **variation**

> You can refer to the Coursebook, but you must write your summary **in your own words.**

....

....

....

....

....

....

....

....

....

....

....

....

....

....

....

2 In Darwin's time, no one knew anything about cell nuclei, chromosomes or genes.

Write a letter to Darwin, explaining to him how his theory is supported by the knowledge that we now have about these and their role in inheritance.

....

....

....

....

....

....

....

....

....

....

....

....

....

....

....

....

....

....

....

....

....

Unit 4 Material properties

4.1 What do the numbers tell you?

This challenge task relates to **4.1 The structure of the atom** and **4.2 More about the structure of the atom** from the Coursebook.

> In this challenge task, you will use information from the Periodic Table to identify and describe the structure of different types of atoms.

	metals																1 H hydrogen 1									2 He helium 4

Periodic table:

- metals (white)
- non-metals (shaded)

1 H hydrogen 1										2 He helium 4

3 Li lithium 7	4 Be beryllium 9									5 B boron 11	6 C carbon 12	7 N nitrogen 14	8 O oxygen 16	9 F fluorine 19	10 Ne neon 20
11 Na sodium 23	12 Mg magnesium 24									13 Al aluminium 27	14 Si silicon 28	15 P phosphorus 31	16 S sulfur 32	17 Cl chlorine 35	18 Ar argon 40
19 K potassium 39	20 Ca calcium 40														

1 What does the atomic number tell you about an element?

   ....

2 What does the mass number tell you about an element?

   ....

3 As you move along a row in the Periodic Table from left to right, and then along the next row, the atomic number and the mass number increase.

   Look carefully. Describe these increases.

   The atomic number ....

   ....

   The mass number ....

   ....

4 Which two elements have the same mass number?

   ....

5 Complete the table of information about the element aluminium.

Element	Aluminium
atomic number	
mass number	
number of protons	
number of neutrons	
number of electrons	
arrangement of electrons	

6 Name an element that is a gas and has the same number of neutrons as protons.

....

7 Complete the table and identify the element.

Element	
atomic number	
mass number	
number of protons	19
number of neutrons	20
number of electrons	
arrangement of electrons	

8 Describe the atomic structure of sodium and compare it to that of lithium.

....

....

....

....

....

....

4.2 Atomic structure and trends

This challenge task relates to **4.4 Trends in some other groups** from the Coursebook.

> In this challenge task, you will draw some atomic structures and compare the trends in Group 8 of the Periodic Table.

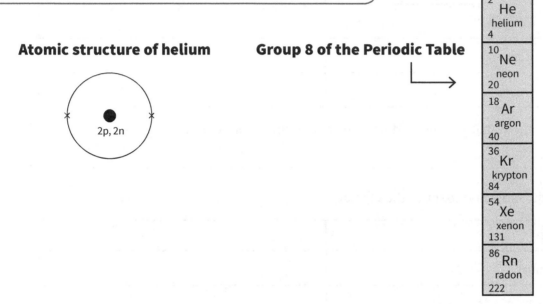

Atomic structure of helium

Group 8 of the Periodic Table

1 Draw atomic structure diagrams for neon and argon.

2 Compare the structures of neon and argon. ....

....

....

....

....

....

3 Use the information in this table to answer the questions below.

Elements in Group 8	Melting point / °C	Boiling point / °C
helium, He	−270	−269
neon, Ne	−249	−246
argon, Ar	−189	−186
krypton, Kr		−153
xenon, Xe	−112	
radon, Rn	−71	−62

a What trend do you see in the melting points and the boiling points as you go down Group 8?

....

....

....

b What do you notice about the melting point and boiling point of each element in Group 8?

....

....

c Predict the melting point of krypton. ....

d Predict the boiling point of xenon. ....

4.3 Comparing the trends in Groups 1 and 7

This challenge task relates to **4.3 Trends in Group 1** and **4.4 Trends in some other groups** from the Coursebook.

> In this challenge task, you will use information to compare elements in the same group.

Group 1

Element	Atomic number	Mass number	Melting point / °C	Boiling point / °C
lithium	3	7	180	1360
sodium	11	23	98	900
potassium	19	39	63	777

Group 7

Element	Atomic number	Mass number	Melting point / °C	Boiling point / °C
fluorine	9	19	−220	−188
chlorine	17	35	−101	−34
bromine	35	80	−7	59

Use the information above to answer the questions.

1 As the atomic number in Group 1 increases, what happens to the melting point?

....

2 As the atomic number in Group 7 increases, what happens to the melting point?
Compare this to what happens in Group 1.

....

....

3 Compare the trends in boiling points in Group 1 and in Group 7.

....

....

....

In Group 1, the least reactive element of those shown on the previous page is lithium; the most reactive is potassium.

In Group 7, the least reactive element of those shown on the previous page is bromine; the most reactive is fluorine.

4 Describe how reactivity relates to the size of the atoms in each group.

In Group 1:

....

....

In Group 7:

....

....

5 The elements that come next in each group, in order of atomic number, are:

- rubidium in Group 1
- iodine in Group 7.

Make predictions about the reactivity, melting point and boiling point of rubidium and iodine, compared with the other elements in their group.

Rubidium, Group 1

Reactivity: ....

Melting point: ....

Boiling point: ....

Iodine, Group 7

Reactivity: ....

Melting point: ....

Boiling point: ....

5.1 Exothermic reactions with metals

This challenge task relates to **5.2 More exothermic reactions** from the Coursebook.

> In this challenge task, you will answer questions about exothermic reactions. Then you will plan an investigation and suggest how to present some results.

When metals in Group 1 of the Periodic Table react with water, a large amount of energy is given out.

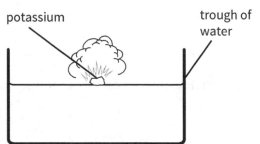

potassium

trough of water

1 Write the word equation for the reaction between potassium and water.

2 What forms of energy are given out from this reaction?

....

....

3 What safety precautions should be taken when carrying out this reaction?

....

....

4 Suggest a way of measuring the energy given out during this reaction.
   Give a reason for your choice.

....

....

....

Metals react with acids to form salts. The general equation is

metal + acid = salt + hydrogen

When this reaction occurs, there is an increase in temperature.

thermometer

dilute hydrochloric acid

magnesium ribbon

5 Explain how you would carry out an investigation to answer the question:

Do different metals produce different increases in temperature when they react with an acid?

....

....

....

....

....

....

....

....

....

....

....

Remember to make your investigation a **fair test**.

Amal investigates the question above using four metals in hydrochloric acid. These are his results.

Metal	Rise in temperature / °C
A	10
B	11
C	14
D	4

6 Which type of graph would you suggest Amal use to present these results? Give a reason for your choice.

....

....

....

5.2 Dissolving potassium chloride

This challenge task relates to **5.3 Endothermic processes** from the Coursebook.

> In this challenge task, you will plan an investigation.

When two or three spatulas of potassium chloride are dissolved in water, the solution formed feels cold. But **no** chemical reaction has taken place.

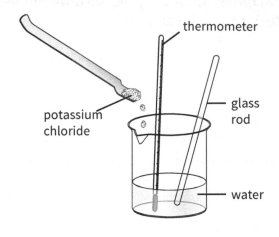

1 Plan an investigation to answer the question:

Does adding more potassium chloride to water produce a lower temperature?

Include an equipment list and write an outline of what you will do.

Include any **preliminary work** you may need to do and why you will do it.

....

....

....

....

....

....

....

....

....

....

....

....

....

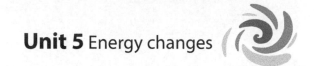
2 Draw a table to record the results of the investigation you planned in question 1.

> You will need to allow for sufficient readings to ensure reliability.

3 Explain the difference between an endothermic **reaction** and an endothermic **process**.

Give one example of each.

....

....

....

....

....

....

5.3 Using exothermic and endothermic reactions

This challenge task relates to **5.4 Exothermic or endothermic?** from the Coursebook.

> In this challenge task, you will explain how exothermic and endothermic reactions and processes are used in everyday life.

Exothermic reactions can be used to make self-heating cans of food.
Calcium oxide and water are often used to produce the rise in temperature.

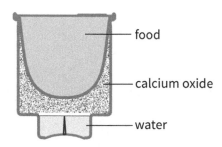

1 Jon does not understand how self-heating cans work. Write a clear explanation for him.

   ....

   ....

   ....

   ....

   ....

2 Suggest why these cans are difficult to manufacture.

   ....

   ....

   ....

3 Suggest when using self-heating cans of food might be useful.

....

....

....

Ice packs are often used when people injure themselves. These are kept in the fridge and placed on the injured area to cool it down. Once the ice has melted they can be returned to the fridge.

Another type of 'cold pack' uses a chemical, which dissolves in water and then the solution gets cooler.

4 Suggest, with reasons, which type of cold pack might be used:

a by a first-aid person on a marathon course

....

....

....

b by a teacher in a school gym.

....

....

....

6.1 How reactive are these metals?

This challenge task relates to **6.3 Reactions of metals with dilute acid**
and **6.4 The reactivity series** from the Coursebook.

> In this challenge task, you will identify variables and practical difficulties
> in an investigation. You will also present and discuss some results.

Anna is asked to investigate the reactivity of six metals with dilute acid.
The metals produce hydrogen when they are added to dilute hydrochloric acid.

The equipment she will use is shown in the diagram.

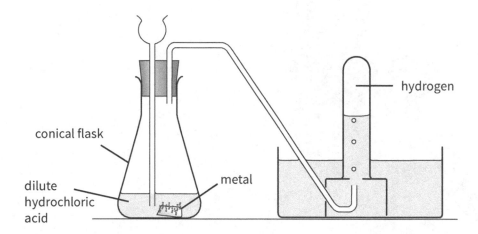

Anna adds a metal to the acid and then times how long it takes to collect a test
tube full of hydrogen.

The metals available are magnesium, zinc, iron, copper, lead and aluminium.

1 Which variables should Anna **control** in order to ensure the test is fair?

State **at least three**.

....

....

....

....

Here are Anna's results.

Metal	Time to collect test tube of hydrogen / s
aluminium	27
zinc	54
magnesium	21
lead	69
iron	49

2 No result for copper is recorded. Suggest why Anna has not included this.

....

....

3 Present these results on the graph grid. Present them in order, with the **least reactive** first.

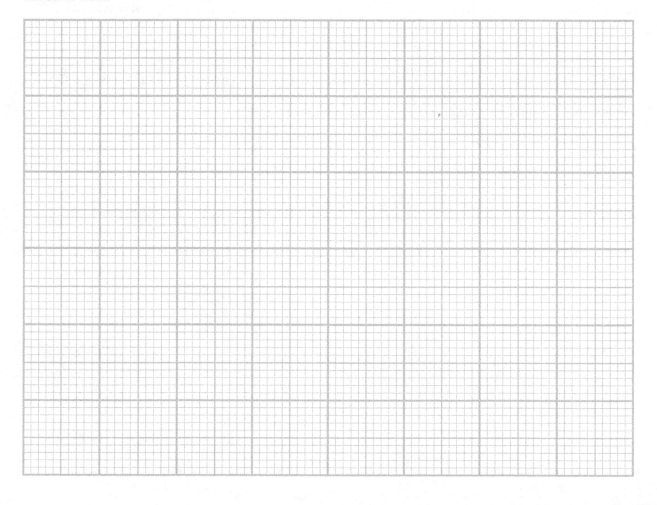

4 Which of Anna's results does not fit the pattern you would expect? Explain your reasoning.

> You may need to look at the reactivity series in your Coursebook.

....

....

....

5 Suggest how Anna could have obtained this odd result.

....

....

....

6 Explain the practical difficulties in using this method to obtain **accurate** results.

....

....

....

....

7 Suggest how Anna could improve the accuracy of her results.

....

....

....

....

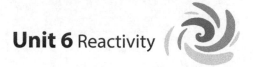

6.2 Which metal?

This challenge task relates to **6.4 The reactivity series** and **6.5 Displacement reactions** from the Coursebook.

> In this challenge task, you will use your knowledge of the reactions of metals to try to identify the metal used.

1 Suggest a metal that burns brightly in air to form an oxide, and has a vigorous reaction in cold water to form a hydroxide.

   ....

2 Suggest a metal that has no reaction with steam, water or dilute acid.

   ....

3 Suggest a metal that will displace copper from a solution of copper sulfate.

   ....

4 Name a metal that burns brightly in air to form an oxide, has a slow reaction in cold water to form a hydroxide, and reacts vigorously with dilute acid.

   ....

5 Write the word equation to show the displacement of iron from iron chloride.

6 Suggest a metal that reacts with steam but not with cold water, to form an oxide.

   ....

7 Name a metal that is more reactive than lead but less reactive than aluminium.

   ....

6.3 Displacing metals

This challenge task relates to **6.4 The reactivity series** and **6.5 Displacement reactions** from the Coursebook.

> In this challenge task, you will discuss the reactivity of metals and predict which displacement reactions will take place.

Sam has six metals, A, B, C, D, E and F. He also has six test tubes of a solution of a salt of metal A, six tubes of a solution of a salt of metal B, and so on.

He adds a small piece of each metal to six tubes, one of each of the salt solutions.

The bar chart shows the number of displacement reactions that take place.

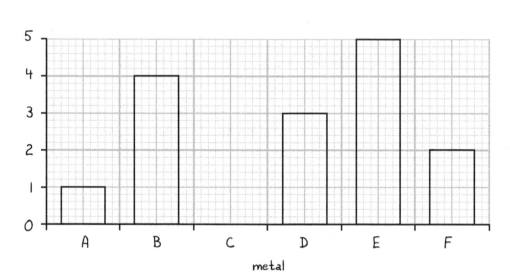

1 Which of the metals A, B, C, D, E, F is the most reactive? Explain your choice.

....

....

....

2 Complete the table on the next page, using Sam's results. Use a tick to show where a displacement reaction has happened, and a cross where a reaction has not happened.

	Metal					
		A	B	C	D	E	F
Metal salt A							
B							
C							
D							
E							
F							

> Start filling in the table for the most reactive metal first, then the next most reactive, and so on.

3 Metal C is copper and metal D is zinc. Suggest what the other metals might be. Give reasons for your choices.

> You may need to look at the reactivity series in your Coursebook.

....

....

....

....

4 Complete the following word equations.

If there is no reaction between the metal and the salt, write 'no reaction'.

a copper sulfate + iron ⟶ ....

b magnesium chloride + zinc ⟶ ....

c aluminium sulfate + magnesium ⟶ ....

d lead chloride + silver ⟶ ....

e zinc chloride + iron ⟶ ....

5 Explain why it is not possible for you to carry out displacement reactions using the metal potassium.

....

....

6.4 Making use of displacement reactions

This challenge task relates to **6.6 Using displacement reactions** from the Coursebook.

> In this challenge task, you will explain how displacement reactions are used in practical ways.

1 Explain how the displacement of iron from iron oxide is used to weld rails together.

....

....

....

....

2 Why is this method used and not ordinary welding?

....

....

3 Write the word equation for this reaction.

Iron is produced from its ore, iron oxide, by using a displacement reaction.
This is done in a blast furnace.

4 Which element is used to displace the iron? ....

5 Describe briefly how this process is carried out.

....

....

6 Write the word equation for this reaction.

7 Suggest where the element used in this reaction fits in the reactivity series.

....

Unit 7 Salts

7.1 Investigating concentration

This challenge task relates to **7.4 Forming salts by neutralisation** from the Coursebook.

> In this challenge task, you will discuss variables in an investigation and make some conclusions from experimental results.

Elsa was asked to investigate this question:

Is there a link between the concentration of acid and the volume of it needed to neutralise 50 cm³ of alkali?

She made up five samples of acid with different concentrations, 100 cm³ of each.

The first sample was from the laboratory bottle of acid.

The second sample was made by adding 50 cm³ of acid to 50 cm³ water.

Each subsequent sample of acid was half the concentration of the previous one.

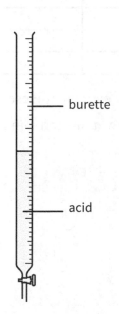

For each sample, Elsa put the acid in a burette and gradually added it to the alkali, until a neutral solution was formed.

1 How could Elsa determine the pH of the solution, and what would she observe as it became neutral?

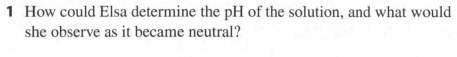

....

....

....

2 Which variables should Elsa have **controlled** to make this a fair test? State **at least three**.

....

....

....

....

3 Here are the results of Elsa's investigation.

Acid sample	Volume of laboratory acid used to make up 100 cm³ diluted sample / cm³	Volume of acid sample needed to neutralise alkali / cm³
A	100	21
B	50	25
C	25	34
D	12.5	51
E	6.25	100

Sample A is the **most concentrated** and sample E is the **least concentrated**.

Plot a graph of these results. Label each plotted point A, B, C, D or E.

Draw a line through the points appropriately.

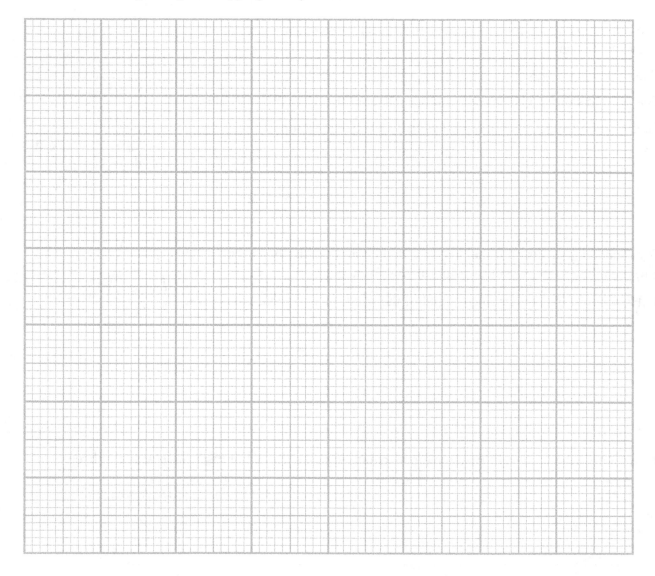

4 Describe the graph.

....

....

5 What **conclusion** can you make from these results?

....

....

....

....

6 Elsa's results were for $50\,cm^3$ of alkali.

Nor did the same investigation but made a mistake. She used $60\,cm^3$ of alkali.

How would Nor's results be affected?

....

....

....

....

7 State the dangers of using concentrated acid, and describe the **safety precautions** that should be taken.

....

....

....

....

....

7.2 Salts, alkalis and equations

This challenge task relates to **7.1 What is a salt?**, **7.2 Preparing a salt using metal and acid**, **7.3 Metal carbonates and acids** and **7.4 Forming salts by neutralisation** from the Coursebook.

In this challenge task, you will use your knowledge to name salts, a base and an alkali. You will also correct some formulae and write word equations.

1 Name a salt formed from the following:

   a hydrochloric acid ....

   b citric acid ....

   c zinc and nitric acid ....

   d copper and sulfuric acid ....

2 These formulae are incorrect. Write them correctly.

   HSO_4 HCl_2 HNO^3

3 Give an example of a base. ....

4 Give an example of an alkali. ....

5 Explain how alkalis and bases are related.

   ....

   ....

6 Write a word equation for the reaction between sulfuric acid and the alkali that contains sodium.

7 Write a word equation for the reaction to prepare the salt copper chloride from copper carbonate.

7.3 Mystery substances

This challenge task relates to **7.1 What is a salt?**, **7.2 Preparing a salt using metal and acid**, **7.3 Metal carbonates and acids** and **7.4 Forming salts by neutralisation** from the Coursebook.

> In this challenge task, you will use the information given to identify some substances.

Jon and Nor had three different substances, **A**, **B** and **C**, each in the form of ground-up powder.

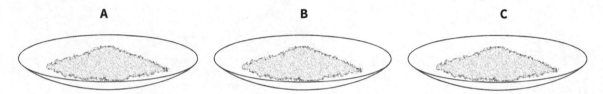

They placed a sample of each in one of three different test tubes.

They added a **different** liquid to each test tube.

They observed the reactions and did some tests.

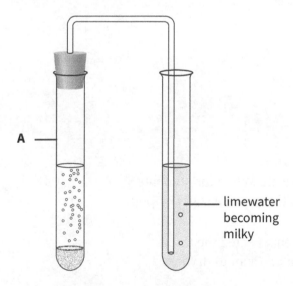

limewater becoming milky

In the tube containing **A**, bubbles of gas were produced. When this gas was passed through limewater, it became milky.

In the tube containing **B**, no bubbles were produced.

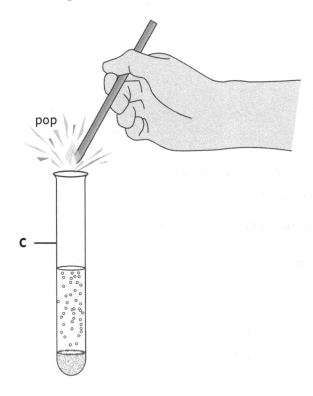

pop

In the tube containing **C,** bubbles of gas were produced. When the students collected this gas and tested it with a lighted splint, there was a squeaky pop.

After the substances had finished reacting, the students heated the three solutions (after filtering if necessary). They evaporated them to dryness to form three crystalline substances:

- substance **A** produced **zinc sulfate**
- substance **B** produced **iron chloride**
- substance **C** produced **magnesium chloride**.

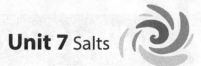

1 Which **gas** did substance **A** produce? ....

2 Which **gas** did substance **C** produce? ....

3 What general name is given to the crystalline substances produced in this way, after evaporation?

....

4 Suggest which **liquid** was added to tube **A**.

....

5 Suggest which **liquid** was added to tube **B**.

....

6 Suggest which **liquid** was added to tube **C**.

....

7 Suggest what substance **A** could have been.

....

8 Suggest what substance **B** could have been.

....

9 Suggest what substance **C** could have been.

....

10 Write a word equation for the reaction involving substance **A**.

11 Write a word equation for the reaction involving substance **B**.

12 Write a word equation for the reaction involving substance **C**.

8.1 Magnesium and hydrochloric acid

This challenge task relates to **8.2 Changes in the rate of reaction** and **8.3 Surface area and the rate of reaction** from the Coursebook.

> In this challenge task, you will plot a graph, predict results and explain your reasons for the prediction.

Nor wanted to investigate the rate of reaction between magnesium ribbon and hydrochloric acid. She collected hydrogen gas and measured its volume every 30 seconds.

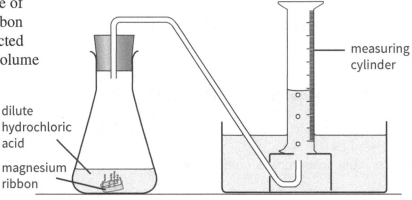

Nor's results are shown here.

1 Plot these results on the graph grid on the next page. Label the line **magnesium ribbon**.

2 Describe what the graph shows.

....

....

....

....

....

....

....

....

....

Time / s	Total volume of hydrogen collected / cm³
0	0
30	10
60	18
90	26
120	29
150	33
180	36
210	38
240	39
270	41
300	41
330	41
360	41
390	41
420	41

3 Explain, using collision theory, why the graph is this shape.

....

....

....

....

....

....

4 Nor repeated the investigation using the same mass of magnesium but in powder form.

What do you **predict** happened? Sketch a line on your graph on the previous page and label the line **magnesium powder**.

5 Explain, using collision theory, why you have drawn the graph this shape.

....

....

....

....

....

....

6 Nor repeated the investigation again, this time using a lump of magnesium of the same mass.

Sketch on your graph what you predict happened. Label the line **lump of magnesium**.

7 Explain, using collision theory, why you have drawn the graph this shape.

....

....

....

....

....

....

8.2 Which results are which?

This challenge task relates to **8.5 Concentration and the rate of reaction** from the Coursebook.

> In this challenge task, you will identify sets of results, and describe, compare and explain the results.

Sam carried out an investigation of the rate of reaction between zinc and sulfuric acid, using different concentrations of acid.

The concentrations he used are shown in the table.

The hydrogen gas produced was collected and its volume measured every 30 seconds.

Concentration	Volume of acid used / cm^3	Volume of water used / cm^3
x5	50	0
x4	40	10
x3	30	20
x2	20	30
x1	10	40
x0	0	50

1 The acid concentration ×0 was not used in the investigation. Why?

    ....

    ....

2 The graph on the next page shows Sam's results for **×4 concentration**, **×3 concentration** and **×2 concentration**.

   Sam has not labelled the concentrations on the graph.

   Label each line with the appropriate concentration.

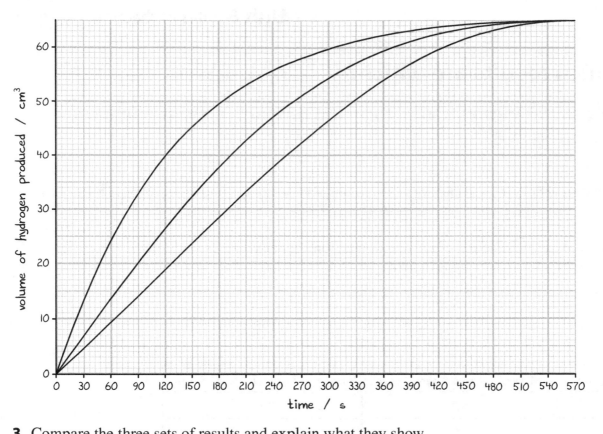

3 Compare the three sets of results and explain what they show.

....

....

....

....

....

....

4 Explain the three sets of results shown on the graph, using particle and collision theory.

....

....

....

....

....

5 Sketch on the same graph your predicted line for the **×5 concentration**. Label the line.

8.3 As fast as possible

This challenge task relates to **8.1 Measuring the rate of reaction**, **8.2 Changes in the rate of reaction**, **8.3 Surface area and the rate of reaction**, **8.4 Temperature and the rate of reaction** and **8.5 Concentration and the rate of reaction** from the Coursebook.

> In this challenge task, you will plan an experiment and explain the reasons for your decisions.

Amal and Anna have been asked to carry out the reaction between marble chips and dilute acid, and to collect $100\,cm^3$ of carbon dioxide in the shortest possible time.

They may only use $20\,g$ of marble chips and $50\,cm^3$ of standard dilute hydrochloric acid. They have access to a range of laboratory equipment.

1 Draw and label a diagram to show how they could carry out this reaction and collect the gas.

2 List all other equipment **not** shown in the diagram that they will need to use.

  ....

  ....

  ....

3 Which variables are the students **not** permitted to change?

....

....

4 Which **two** variables could they change to give a faster rate of reaction?

Variable 1: ....

Variable 2: ....

5 Explain, for each of the variables you have stated in question 4, how changing it will speed up the rate of reaction.

Variable 1:

....

....

....

....

....

Variable 2:

....

....

....

....

....

6 Describe how Anna and Amal should carry out this experiment.

....

....

....

....

....

....

....

....

....

....

....

....

....

....

7 Suggest practical difficulties in carrying out this experiment, which may make the collection time longer than it should be.

....

....

....

....

....

....

....

....

....

....

....

....

....

....

Unit 9 Forces in action

9.1 Density problems

This challenge task relates to **9.2 Measuring density** and **9.3 Density calculations** from the Coursebook.

> In this challenge task, you will plan an investigation about density, make some estimates and do some calculations.

Anna wants to find the density of a small piece of rock about 2 cm across.

She has the equipment shown.

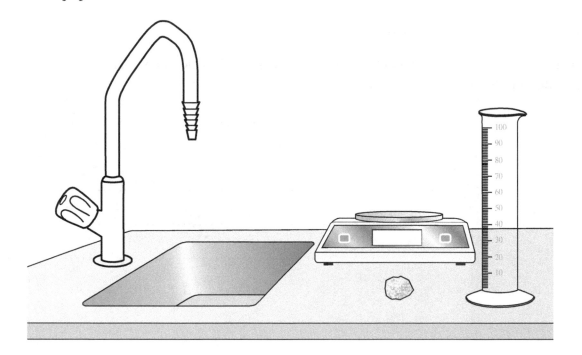

1 Describe how Anna can use this equipment to find the density of the rock.
   She wants the unit of density to be g/cm³.

   ....

   ....

   ....

   ....

   ....

   ....

2 Anna finds the density of the piece of rock is 2.7 g/cm^3.

Suggest why the density of another piece of the **same** type of rock could be slightly different.

....

....

3 Anna has a different rock, which has a density of 4.2 g/cm^3. It has a mass of 230 g.

Calculate the volume of this piece of rock. Give your answer to two significant figures.

> First write down the formula you will use. Show your working.

............cm^3

4 Sam has a toy made of wood with some metal parts.

The toy has an irregular shape. The largest dimension is 12 cm and the smallest dimension is 8 cm.

The toy floats when put into water.

Describe how Sam could find the volume of the toy.

....

....

....

....

....

5 Without measuring, **estimate** the length, width and height of your classroom.

Estimate each dimension as a whole number.

length ....m

width ....m

height ....m

6 Use your estimated dimensions to estimate the volume of your classroom.

Show your working.

............m^3

7 The density of air can be estimated as $1\,kg/m^3$.

Use this value to estimate the mass of air in your classroom.

............kg

8 The density of air is lower than $1\,kg/m^3$ at high altitude.

How would your estimate of the mass in question 7 be different at higher altitude?

....

9 The diagram shows the fuel tank in a car.

fuel is put
in here

pipe taking fuel
to the engine   tank

Water can sometimes get into the fuel tank. If the
water in the fuel tank reaches the engine, the engine
will stop.

The density of the fuel is $0.75\,g/cm^3$.
The density of water is $1.00\,g/cm^3$.
Water does **not** mix with the fuel.

Suggest why the pipe from the tank to the engine does **not** come
from the bottom of the tank. Use the information in the box.

....

....

....

9.2 Applying pressure

This challenge task relates to **9.5 Pressure calculations** and **9.6 Pressure in gases and liquids** from the Coursebook.

> In this challenge task, you will plot a graph, make conclusions from results and do some calculations. You will also consider the difficulties involved with some scientific research.

Jon is investigating how pressure affects air in a syringe.

He clamps a large syringe vertically and seals the opening of the syringe.

When he puts a load on the plunger, it goes down as shown in the diagram.

Jon puts different loads on the plunger and records the volume of air each time.

His results are shown in the table.

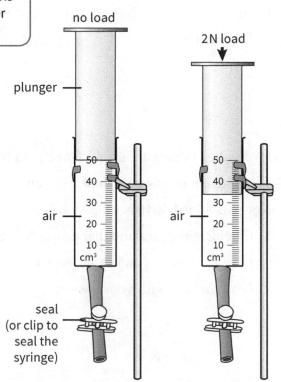

Load / N	Volume of air / cm³
2	
4	18
6	12
8	9
10	7

1 Use information from the diagram to complete the table for the load of 2 N.

2 Plot a graph of Jon's results on the grid. Put **load** on the *x*-axis and **volume of air** on the *y*-axis.

   Draw a smooth curve through your points.

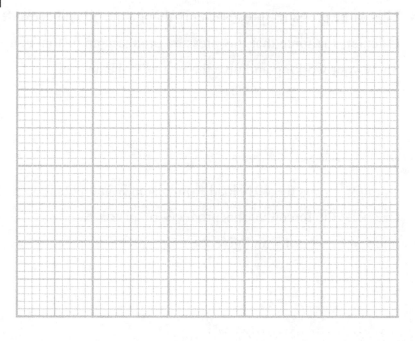

3 Describe the pattern in Jon's results.

....

....

....

4 Jon's teacher tells him that the volume of air in the syringe will **never** reach zero.

Explain this.

....

....

Hydraulic systems are used in machines to produce different forces.

The diagram shows a hydraulic system.

Nor puts a load of 10 N on piston **X**.

5 Calculate the pressure that piston **X** exerts on the oil.

Give the formula and show your working.

Give the unit with your answer.

piston X
area = 4 cm²

oil

piston Y
area = 16 cm²

....

6 This **same** pressure spreads evenly though the oil and is exerted on piston **Y**.

Calculate the force that this pressure produces on piston **Y**.

Show your working and give the unit with the answer.

....

7 Nor now moves the 10 N load from piston **X** and puts it on piston **Y**.

Calculate the force that this produces on piston **X**.

Show your working and give the unit with the answer.

....

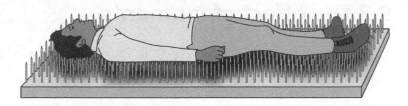

Elsa goes to a fair.

She sees a man lying on a bed of nails.

The bed is made from wood and there are thousands of nails pointing upwards through the wood.

When the man gets off the bed, he has no injuries from the nails.

8 Explain, in terms of pressure, how it is possible for the man to lie on thousands of nails without injury, although lying on just one nail would cause injury.

....

....

....

9 Elsa notices that the man rolls off the bed – he does not sit up before getting off.

Explain, in terms of pressure, why he does not sit up on the bed.

....

....

....

A submarine is a type of ship that is designed to travel **under** water. Scientists use submarines to research the oceans.

Very little research has been done in the deepest parts of the oceans. This is because of the very high cost of the submarines.

10 Suggest why it is much more expensive to build submarines to go into the deepest parts of the oceans, than those that go to shallower parts.

....

....

....

11 To get the money for research, scientists must apply to governments or companies.

Suggest **two** reasons why it is more difficult to get the money for ocean research than for medical research.

....

....

9.3 The effect of moments

This challenge task relates to **9.8 The principle of moments** and **9.9 Calculating moments** from the Coursebook.

> In this challenge task, you will make calculations and predictions about moments.

The diagram shows a barrier at a railway crossing.

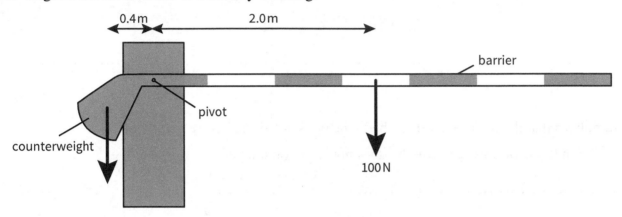

1 Calculate the moment about the pivot caused by the weight of the barrier.

Show your working.

.... N m

2 Calculate the force required from the counterweight to balance the barrier.

Show your working.

.... N

3 Suggest why the counterweight is slightly smaller than is required to exactly balance the barrier. Explain your answer.

....

....

....

4 The human arm operates as a lever.

The diagram shows the arm supporting a 10 N load.

Calculate the moment about the elbow caused by holding the load.

Show your working.

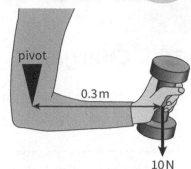

.... N m

5 This picture shows a woman doing a balancing act. She is **not** moving.

On the drawing, mark the position of the pivot with a triangle (△).

6 Explain why the woman's left arm is extended.

....

....

....

7 The woman now bends her knees to bring her feet upwards, but does not move any other part of her body.

Suggest what would happen and explain your reasoning.

....

....

....

8 Tower Bridge in London has two sections that can be raised to allow ships to pass.

The diagram shows one half of the bridge with its section lowered.

The weight of the section is 10 000 000 N.

The moment produced by this weight is 150 000 000 N m.

Calculate distance d.

Show your working and give the unit.

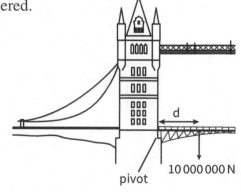

....

Unit 10 Electricity

10.1 Charge

This challenge task relates to **10.2 Positive and negative charge** and **10.3 Electrons on the move** from the Coursebook.

> In this challenge task, you will consider how scientists work, and how they have identified the particles inside an atom. You will also consider some effects of static electricity.

About 2600 years ago, a Greek scientist called Thales rubbed amber against fur.

He noticed that the amber could then attract small hairs from the fur.

1 By doing this, what had Thales made?
Tick **one** box.

a hypothesis ☐   an observation ☐

a prediction ☐   a conclusion ☐

2 What caused the hairs to be attracted to the amber?
Tick **all** that apply.

like charges ☐   a non-contact force ☐   gravity ☐

opposite charges ☐   magnetism ☐   static electricity ☐

3 Suggest why Thales could **not** explain why the hairs were attracted to the amber.

....

4 In the 1890s, a British scientist called Thomson discovered the electron.

Suggest why there was such a long time between Thales' experiment and Thomson's discovery.

....

....

....

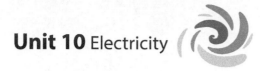
The diagram shows an atom.

5 On the diagram, label the parts of the atom.

6 Beside each label, write the type of charge of that part.

7 What happens to a substance when it becomes positively charged?
Tick **one** box.

electrons move on ☐   positive charges move on ☐

electrons move off ☐   positive charges move off ☐

8 When fuel such as gasoline or diesel flows through rubber pipes, charge can build up in the fuel.

Fuel systems need to be designed to **stop** charge building up.

Suggest why charge building up in fuel could be dangerous.

....

....

9 The diagram shows what happens when a thundercloud is over a tree.

Lightning strikes from the cloud to the tree.

State the direction that negative charges move in this lightning strike.

....

....

10 Lightning causes some atoms in the air to lose electrons.

What charge will remain on a particle that has lost electrons?
Tick **one** box.

no charge ☐

positive ☐

negative ☐

10.2 Current in circuits

This challenge task relates to **10.4 Conductors and insulators, 10.5 Electric current in a circuit**, **10.7 Changing circuits 1** and **10.8 Changing circuits 2** from the Coursebook.

> In this challenge task, you will consider the functions of components in a circuit, the nature of current and the effect of varying resistance.

1 Complete the table by writing the name of the component, drawing its circuit symbol or stating its function.

Name of component	Circuit symbol	Function of component
cell		
lamp		
wire		to conduct current through other components
open switch		to stop the flow of current

2 Complete the sentences using the words from the list.

Each word can be used once, more than once or not at all.

amps   complete   energy   faster   slower

The battery in a circuit provides a supply of ....

Current can only flow in .... circuits.

Current is measured in ....

A higher current in a circuit means .... is delivered

.... to components.

Nor builds the circuit shown below.

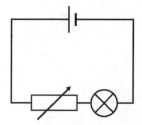

She sets the variable resistor so it has **minimum** resistance.

3 Describe what changes Nor can see in the circuit as she slides the contact on the variable resistor to the other end.

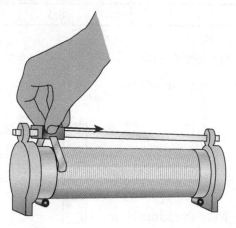

....

10.3 Different types of circuit

This challenge task relates to **10.8 Changing circuits 2** and **10.9 Components in parallel** from the Coursebook.

In this challenge task, you will consider current in different types of circuit, including parallel arrangements. You will also draw a graph of voltage against current and design a circuit.

Anna has a circuit with two lamps.

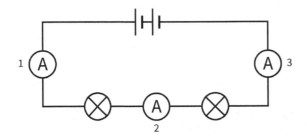

The reading on one of the ammeters is 0.3 A.

1 Which row in the table shows the correct readings on all three ammeters?

Circle **one** letter, **X**, **Y** or **Z**.

	Reading on meter 1 / A	Reading on meter 2 / A	Reading on meter 3 / A
X	0.1	0.2	0.3
Y	0.3	0.2	0.1
Z	0.3	0.3	0.3

2 Anna now disconnects the battery from her circuit.

What happens to the readings on the three ammeters?
Tick **one** box.

Ammeter 1 will drop to zero first. ☐

Ammeter 3 will drop to zero first. ☐

Ammeters 1, 2 and 3 will drop to zero at the same time. ☐

Explain your answer.

....

....

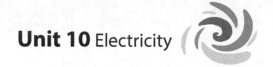

Elsa set up this circuit.

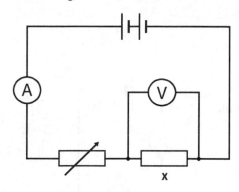

3 Complete the sentences by using the words **series** or **parallel**.

The voltmeter is connected in ……………………………… with component **X**.

The ammeter is connected in ……………………………… with component **X**.

Elsa used the variable resistor to change the current through component **X**.

She recorded the readings from the ammeter and voltmeter in this table.

4 Complete the table by filling in the final missing voltage reading.

5 Plot a graph of the results on the grid below.

Current / A	Voltage / V
0.1	1.5
0.2	3.0
0.3	4.5
0.4	6.0
0.5	

- Put current on the x-axis.
- Start both axes at zero.
- Draw a line though your points.

6 From your graph in question 5, predict the voltage when the current is:

a zero ....

b 2A ....

Amal builds a circuit with four lamps, **A** to **D**, shown in this diagram.

7 Complete the sentences using the letters **A, B, C** or **D**.

a Lamps .... and .... are in series with each other.

b Lamps .... and .... are in parallel with each other.

8 Give the letter of the lamp that could break to cause:

a **all** of the others to go off ....

b **none** of the others to go off. ....

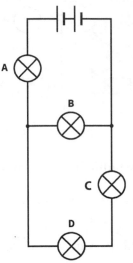

A car has a heated rear window to help remove condensation.

The circuit diagram for the heated rear window is shown.

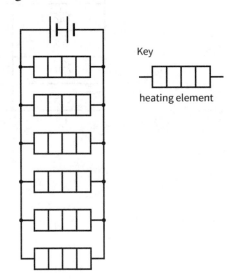

Key

heating element

The current through **each** heating element is 1.0A.

9 Write down the **total** current supplied by the battery. ....

10 Write on the circuit diagram for the heated rear window (on the previous page):

- the letter **X** where **one** switch could be placed to turn off **all** the heating elements

- the letter **Y** where **one** switch could be placed to turn off **three** of the heating elements.

11 Suggest **one** advantage of having the heating elements connected in parallel rather than in series.

....

....

12 The heated rear window in most cars automatically switches off after about ten minutes.

Suggest why.

....

....

Jon has a battery, wires, switches and three lamps.

He wants to build a circuit in which each of the three lamps can be switched on or off, independently of the others.

13 Draw a circuit diagram for this in the space below.

Unit 11 Energy

11.1 Energy and fuel

This challenge task relates to **11.1 How we use energy**, **11.2 Fossil fuels** and **11.3 Renewables and non-renewables** from the Coursebook.

> In this challenge task, you will describe and explain trends in energy use.

1 Name the **three** types of fossil fuel.

....

2 Explain why fossil fuels are described as 'non-renewable'.

....

....

The two pie charts show the sources of energy used for electricity generation in part of Canada in 2010 and 2015.

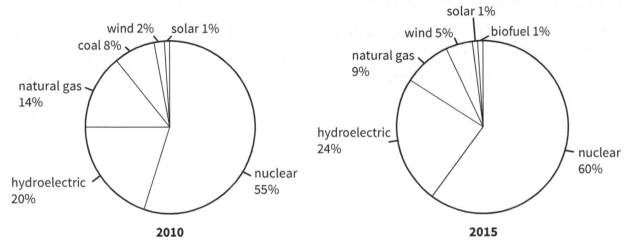

2010   **2015**

Use the information in the pie charts to answer these questions.

3 Name a source of energy that was:

    a used in 2010 but not used in 2015 ....

    b not used in 2010 but used in 2015. ....

4 Name the source of energy that did not change in use between 2010 and 2015.

....

5 Calculate the percentage of energy that came from renewable sources in 2010 and in 2015. Show your working.

2010:   2015:

…………% …………%

6 Suggest what could happen to the percentage of energy coming from renewable sources in the future. Give **two** reasons for your answer.

……………………………………………………………………………………………………

……………………………………………………………………………………………………

……………………………………………………………………………………………………

7 Give **one disadvantage** of relying on wind as a source of energy.

……………………………………………………………………………………………………

8 As countries become more developed, the amount of energy they use increases. Give **three** reasons for this.

……………………………………………………………………………………………………

……………………………………………………………………………………………………

……………………………………………………………………………………………………

9 Energy use per person in the USA is higher than the global average.

What additional information would be needed to show whether energy use in the USA is **increasing faster** than the global average is increasing?

> The **global average** energy use per person is the average energy use per person for all countries in the world.

……………………………………………………………………………………………………

……………………………………………………………………………………………………

……………………………………………………………………………………………………

……………………………………………………………………………………………………

11.2 Conduction

This challenge task relates to **11.4 Conduction of heat** from the Coursebook.

> In this challenge task, you will consider how thermal energy is transferred.
> You will also describe variables in an investigation and draw a results table.

Sam holds an ice cube in his hand. It feels cold.

1 Complete the table by writing the words **true** or **false** next to each statement.

Statement	True or false
Thermal energy moves from Sam's hand into the ice cube.	
Cold moves from the ice cube into Sam's hand.	
The movement of energy occurs by conduction.	
The ice will melt and the water in Sam's hand will reach the same temperature as his hand.	
The ice will melt and the water in Sam's hand will become warmer than his hand.	

Elsa is investigating conduction of heat through different materials.

The diagram shows her investigation.

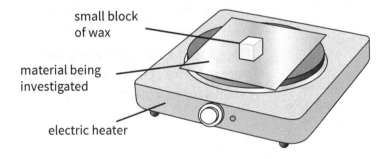

small block
of wax

material being
investigated

electric heater

The electric heater is cold at the start.

Elsa puts different materials between the electric heater and the block of wax.

2 Describe what Elsa will see when she puts a good thermal conductor between the electric heater and the block of wax, then turns the electric heater on.

....

....

3 Describe the **safety precautions** that Elsa needs to take during this investigation.

....

....

....

4 Elsa wants to test four different materials to compare their ability to conduct heat.

a State the **dependent** variable for this investigation.

....

b List variables that need to be **controlled** during this investigation.

....

....

....

c Draw a table suitable for Elsa to record her results.

d Explain why a line graph is **not** a suitable way to present results of this investigation.

....

....

11.3 Investigating heat loss

This challenge task relates to **11.4 Conduction of heat** and **11.5 Convection** from the Coursebook.

> In this challenge task, you will explain the process of convection, plan an investigation and sketch a graph.

1 Explain why convection can occur in liquids and gases but not in solids.

....

....

....

Anna is investigating heat loss from a wooden box.

She puts a lamp inside the box to use as a heat source. She also puts a thermometer in the box to measure the temperature.

There is **no** lid on the box.

After five minutes, she turns the lamp off.

She records the temperature in the box every 30 seconds.

2 State the **dependent** and the **independent** variables in this investigation.

dependent: ....

independent: ....

Anna repeats the experiment, this time **with a lid** on the box.

The lid has a small hole to allow the thermometer to fit though. So she does **not** have to remove the lid to record the temperature.

3 On the grid on the next page, sketch the shape of the two graphs you would expect for the temperature changing with time.

Label your curves 'no lid' and 'with lid'.

You should draw and label axes, but you need not put numbers on the axes.

temperature of
the room

Anna wants to use this apparatus to test the effect of lids of different materials
on the rate at which the box loses heat.

She has lids made of these materials:

- wood
- card
- iron
- plastic.

4 Plan an investigation that Anna could do to test each lid.

Remember to state variables that she should measure and variables that she
should control.

....

....

....

....

....

....

....

....

....

....

11.4 Investigating radiation

This challenge task relates to **11.4 Conduction of heat**, **11.5 Convection**, **11.6 Radiation** and **11.7 Evaporation** from the Coursebook.

> In this challenge task, you will describe how to increase the reliability of an investigation and consider the practical application of results.

1 Name the type of radiation that transfers thermal energy. ....

2 Describe the surface that is the best absorber of this radiation.

  ....

3 Explain why radiation can travel through a vacuum, but conduction and convection **cannot** occur in a vacuum.

  ....

  ....

  ....

When food is cooked in an oven that is not a microwave oven, the food is sometimes wrapped in aluminium foil.

Aluminium foil is made with a shiny side and a dull side.

4 Explain which way round the foil should be used to wrap the food so that it cooks more quickly.

  ....

  ....

  ....

  ....

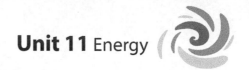
Jon is investigating how colours affect radiation of thermal energy.

He uses five metal cans, which he paints in different colours.

Jon puts hot water in each and measures the temperature every minute.

Jon keeps the following variables constant:

- type of can
- volume of water
- temperature of the room
- draughts in the room
- the surface that the cans are on
- type of paint.

5 State **one other** variable that must be kept constant in this investigation.

....

6 Thermal energy is lost from the water in other ways, not only by radiation from the sides of the metal can. This makes the results less reliable.

Draw a table to show the other methods of heat transfer from the water, where this happens and how these heat losses can be reduced.

Jon's cans in the experiment on the previous page are painted in the following colours:

- red
- yellow
- blue
- black
- white.

None of them is shiny.

7 Which of these colours will he find is:

a the **best** radiator of thermal energy? ....

b the **worst** radiator of thermal energy? ....

8 Central heating radiators are usually painted white.

State which colour would be better in terms of thermal radiation. Suggest why this colour is **not** used.

....

....

9 Some people put aluminium foil between their central heating radiators and the wall of the room. Suggest why they do this.

....

....

10 The Sun radiates thermal energy.

Suggest how the average temperature of planets in the Solar System varies with distance from the Sun.

....

....

11 Explain the trend you described in question 10.

....

....

11.5 Investigating evaporation

This challenge task relates to **11.7 Evaporation** from the Coursebook.

> In this challenge task, you will plan an investigation. You will also explain how evaporation is used for cooling water, air and people.

Nor makes a **hypothesis**.

I think that water will evaporate faster if the temperature of the water is higher.

She has the following equipment:

- distilled (pure) water
- 50 cm³ beakers
- 50 cm³ measuring cylinders

- a digital balance
- a thermometer
- a stopwatch

- a 30 cm ruler
- a Bunsen burner, tripod and gauze.

1 Plan an investigation method that Nor can use to test her hypothesis.

Your plan should contain sufficient information for someone else to follow the method exactly **and safely**. You do not have to use all the equipment.

....

....

....

....

....

....

....

....

....

....

....

2 If Nor followed your plan, what **evidence** would confirm her hypothesis?

....

....

3 Use ideas about evaporation to answer the following questions.

  a The diagram shows a simple type of air cooler.

     The fan blows air through a wet filter.

vent for air to come out

filter soaked in water

electric fan

container of water to keep filter wet

Explain why the air is cooler after it passes though the filter.

....

....

  b The picture shows a water cooler that is used in hot countries.

     The container is filled with water.

     The clay in the sides of the container is porous and lets water soak through to the outside.

     Explain how this can cool the water inside the container.

....

....

  c Explain why, when a person sweats, they cool faster when the wind blows than when the wind does not blow.

....

....